CCSS Genre Play

MW00567389

Essential Question
How do you decide what is important?

THE NAMING OF
ATHENS
A PLAY

by Dawn McMillan
illustrated by Maxim Larin

THE NAMING OF ATHENS

Characters

Reader

Cecrops, a half-man, half-serpent, who will be the king of the new city

Gods and Goddesses of Olympia, including:
Zeus, king of the gods
Poseidon, god of the sea
Athena, goddess of wisdom

Citizen One

Other Citizens

List of Props

Poseidon's trident, a large rock, water jars, an olive seed, an olive tree

The New City

On a rocky hilltop in ancient Greece

READER: Athens was the most powerful city in ancient Greece. The people of Athens had a civilization that is still admired today. This is how the city got its name.

CECROPS: (*to the gods and goddesses*) Gods and goddesses, look at the beautiful land below us. I've named the land after myself, Cecrops. Now I see the beginnings of a wonderful new city. The new city should be called Cecrops as well. Don't you all agree?

half-man

half-serpent

Cecrops

GODS AND GODDESSES: (*together*) No! No!

We want to name this new city after one of us.

Call it after me!

No, me!

The city should have *my* name.

I'll name the city.

POSEIDON: Listen, my friends! The city should have my name. I am Poseidon, god of the sea. Everyone knows how powerful the ocean is. This city is surrounded by ocean water. The city should be called Poseidon!

trident

Poseidon

ATHENA: Poseidon, I can see that you are obsessed with the idea of the city having your name. But I don't think it's a good idea. The ocean can be wild and angry. The city should have a quieter name, like mine. I am the goddess of wisdom. The people in our <u>new</u> city will need to be wise.

POSEIDON: That is nonsense! I...

ZEUS: Wait! Arguing will only bring us anguish. Poseidon, Athena, both of you deserve to have the city named after you. I need to find a way to decide between you. I will ask the thunder to help me.

Zeus

Thunder rolls.

Language Detective	<u>New</u> is an adjective. Find another adjective on this page.

Athena

ZEUS: Gods and goddesses, do not be alarmed! The thunder speaks great wisdom. Poseidon and Athena, you will each bring a gift for the city. Tomorrow we will all meet here again. Bring us the best gift, and the city will be named after you.

GODS OF OLYMPUS: (*together*) Good idea! Bring us your gifts. Tomorrow we will decide.

ZEUS: I think it's necessary for the citizens of the new city to see Poseidon and Athena's gifts. I will send a rainbow to lead them here.

GODS OF OLYMPUS: Yes!

Of course!

The citizens must agree!

Fair enough!

The citizens must decide!

ZEUS: See you tomorrow, then.

rainbow

STOP AND CHECK

How will Zeus decide who the city will be named after?

Scene Two
The Gods' Gifts

READER: The next day, the citizens of the city and the gods of Olympus gathered together.

CECROPS: Welcome! Welcome, everyone! Hello, Zeus. Here, sit by me. It is a good morning. Just a little rain earlier, to help make your rainbow. Now the sun is shining brightly. It is a good day for deciding the name of our new city.

ZEUS: Greetings, all. Gods, goddesses, and citizens… We are here to see the gifts that Poseidon and Athena have brought for our city. Poseidon will present his gift first. Welcome, Poseidon!

Poseidon steps forward and bows. Everyone claps.

POSEIDON: I possess great powers. See the magic that happens when I strike this rock!

Poseidon marches forward and strikes a large rock with his trident, then turns to face the citizens.

Look at the water coming from the rock! Citizens of the new city, I bring you a source of water that will never dry up! Your crops will not dry up and die in the hot summer sun. You will never go thirsty. This gift is a miracle. It is what the city needs!

CITIZEN 1: Is it fresh water?

POSEIDON: Of course! It is fresh, clean water. Taste it for yourselves!

CITIZEN 1: This water tastes terrible! It's salty, like the sea!

CITIZENS: (*tasting the water*)

Dreadful!

Disgusting!

We cannot drink this water!

CITIZEN 1: Poseidon, we can't drink seawater. This will not do! This water is not a <u>suitable gift</u> for our city.

The citizens shake their heads and pour the water from their jars.

> **In Other Words** appropriate present. En español, *suitable gift* quiere decir *un regalo adecuado.*

citizens

CECROPS: Indeed, it will not do!

ZEUS: Poseidon, your power as god of the sea is too strong. Strike the rock again and stop the flow of this salty water!

Poseidon strikes the rock. Then he leaves the stage angrily.

CITIZENS: Athena! Athena! We want Athena!

ZEUS: Yes. Athena, come and show us your gift.

Athena comes to stand in front of the citizens, gods, and goddesses. Everyone is excited to see what Athena will bring.

ZEUS: (*looking confused*) Where is your gift, Athena?

Athena opens her hand to show an olive seed. She turns to face the citizens.

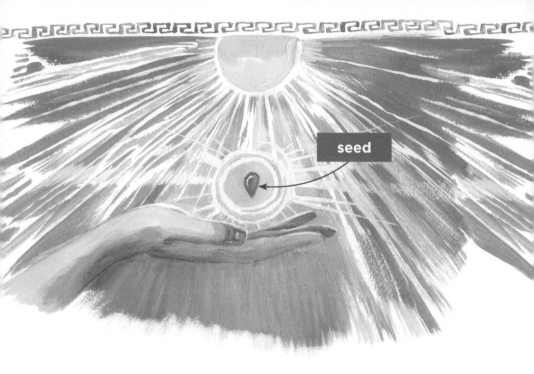

seed

ATHENA: Here is my gift for your city. <u>This</u> olive seed will give you food and oil to cook with. This seed will give you firewood to keep you warm in winter. These things are necessary for a good life in our new city. Watch as I plant this seed.

The citizens, gods, and goddesses gather around as Athena plants the seed in the ground.

ATHENA: See how the seed grows!

An olive tree prop is pushed onto the stage.

| Language Detective | <u>This</u> is a limiting adjective. Can you find another one on this page? |

GODS AND GODDESSES: It is a miracle!

CITIZENS: Incredible!

Everyone claps.

CITIZEN 1: This is a gift we need. It will bring our city wealth. Athena, we will name the city after you.

CITIZENS: Athena! Athena! Athena!

olive tree

ZEUS: Our problem is solved. Cecrops, announce the name of the new city.

CECROPS: Athena, naming the city after you is a great reward for bringing us such a perfect gift! Our new city will be named Athens. We will build beautiful temples and present you with treasure. Our new city is to be called Athens!

CITIZENS: (*dancing around*) Athens! A great name for a new city!

Athena bows, and everyone applauds.

STOP AND CHECK

Why was Poseidon's gift rejected by the citizens and the gods?

Respond to Reading

Summarize

Use details from *The Naming of Athens* to summarize the story. Your graphic organizer may help you.

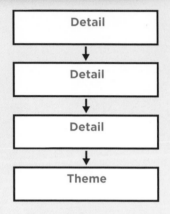

Detail
Detail
Detail
Theme

Text Evidence

1. How can you tell *The Naming of Athens* is a play and a myth? List two things that are special about this kind of text. GENRE

2. What did the citizens think of the gift Poseidon and Athena chose for the citizens? THEME

3. Find the word powerful on page 4. What is the root word of powerful? What do you think the word means? ROOT WORDS

4. Write a new ending to the play in which Poseidon was the winner. What would be different? WRITE ABOUT READING

Compare Texts

Read how Luke finds a perfect present for his mother.

The Perfect Present

The day before Mom's birthday, I went to the mall with my dad.

"I haven't got a clue what to buy for your mother!" Dad said.

I sighed and said, "I don't know what to get either. I've got $5.50. I can't get too many things with my amount of money."

Dad bought a shirt for Mom. I looked in all the shops, but I couldn't find anything. I thought about making a card and buying Mom a bar of soap.

In Other Words I don't know. En español, *I haven't got a clue* quiere decir *no tengo ni remota idea*.

Illustration: Sole Otero

17

On the way home, we went to the grocery store. I found a better present for Mom. I could afford strawberries! Strawberries were my mother's favorite fruit.

Before we left, I paid for the strawberries. At home, I hid the strawberries in my room. I made Mom a beautiful birthday card shaped like a strawberry.

The next morning, I washed the strawberries and put them in a bowl. Then I opened the bedroom door.

"Happy Birthday, Mom," I said. I gave her the strawberries and the card.

Mom sat up. "Strawberries are my favorite! And what a beautiful card!" said Mom.

"Eat your strawberries, Mom, and I'll bring you some coffee," I said. Then I saw Dad's hand move.

"Watch out, Mom!" I yelled. "Dad is after your strawberries!"

Mom laughed. "If Dad helps you make the coffee, I might give him one strawberry," she said.

Dad and I made coffee in the kitchen. Dad said, "You got your mother a great present."

I was really happy I had found something special for my special mom.

Make Connections

In *The Perfect Present,* how did Luke decide what to buy for his mother? ESSENTIAL QUESTION

What helps the citizens in *The Naming of Athens* and Luke in *The Perfect Present* get what they want? TEXT TO TEXT

Focus on Genre

Plays A play is a story that is written to be performed rather than read. The people that perform in a play are called actors. Sets show the audience where the action is taking place. Props, such as the olive tree in *The Naming of Athens*, also help make the story come alive.

Read and Find In *The Naming of Athens*, the names of the characters are written in upper case and bold. A colon separates the name of the character from the words that the character speaks. The stage directions are written in italics. These directions tell the characters what to do.

Your Turn

Imagine if Apollo, the god of the sun, also entered the competition in the play. What gift might he have offered? Write another scene for *The Naming of Athens*. Remember to use text features to show which character is speaking and what the character is saying and doing.